MY 'EXTRA' LIFE
MAGGIE COBBETT

To Heather,

With my very best wishes,

Maggie Cobbett

Copyright 2022 Maggie Cobbett. The right of Maggie Cobbett to be identified as the author of this work has been asserted by her in accordance with the Copyright, Designs and Patents Act 1998. All rights reserved.

No part of this publication may be reproduced, stored in, or introduced into a retrieval system, or transmitted in any form or by any means (electronic, mechanical, photocopying, recording or otherwise) without prior permission.

Published by Guy Richardson

DEDICATION

To all the unsung heroes I met along the way

HOW I GOT STARTED

"What have I seen you in?" is almost always the first thing that people ask when they hear about my 'extra' life. This is usually followed by, "Have you worked with anyone famous?"
The answer to the first question is, "Probably nothing," the nature of the job having been to blend in with the background. To the second, I can truthfully reply, "Yes. Many times."

I used to think the inner workings of film and television closed to all but the lucky few. With drama departments churning out hundreds of hopefuls every year, stardom is certainly hard to achieve, but then I discovered quite by chance that anyone capable of taking direction, available mainly during the working week and willing to travel independently to different locations could apply to be a supporting artist (SA) or 'extra'.

Seen but rarely noticed by an audience focusing on the main action, SAs help to make a scene come to life. Passing through the bar in their local, crossing the street to post a letter or getting off a bus, they're often little more than moving wallpaper and yet the part they play is vital. Imagine a hospital with no flow through of medical staff, patients and visitors or a shop, pub or restaurant with no customers in the background. A sporting fixture needs spectators, a transport hub needs passengers and a police station needs officers and the people they're dealing with. City streets call for crowds, country lanes for hikers and the seaside for holiday makers. These are just a handful of the scenarios that require SAs.

Taking it as a serious endeavour to make big money or an attempt to crack into the industry were equally far from my mind when I first dipped my toe into the water and that's just as well, given that neither of those ever happened. Rather I was looking around for a new challenge and fresh inspiration for my writing when I responded to a newspaper advertisement from a casting agency due to launch in my area. A week later I found myself at a briefing in a large room full of people of all ages, builds and ethnicities. Some were aspiring actors, others veterans of amateur dramatics, but we were told that no previous experience was necessary. Even better, the fledgling agency would demand no joining fee. Its income would come from commission charged on whatever we might earn from the bookings it arranged for us. We were warned about rogue agencies charging outrageous amounts for enrolment and providing very little, if any, work to those lured in by their extravagant promises.

"How much could we earn then?" asked an eager voice and a few faces fell at the reply.

"Well, probably not enough to make a living, unless you're completely free of other commitments, willing to accept bookings at the very last minute and travel – usually under your own steam – as far as required."

On the other hand, we were reassured, pay rates agreed by the actors' union Equity with BBC or ITV were clear cut and kept under review. Everyone in the industry benefited from those agreements, although union membership hadn't been a requirement since the 'closed shop' was made illegal in the early 1990s. SAs didn't qualify for on screen credits or repeat fees, but should be paid for auditions and costume fittings where required. There was even the possibility of earning a few pounds extra for agreeing to an appropriate haircut for a particular scenario. Working at night or on public holidays paid more, scenes involving large crowds slightly less. We were also warned that fees from other production companies would vary but were often considerably lower. It was a lot to take in.

There was a simple application form to complete and a request for a professional 10" by 8" black and white headshot. A few people had arrived already equipped with theirs, but a photographer was on hand to sell his services there and then to those who hadn't. Alternatively, we could make our own arrangements and send in the photographs as soon as possible. The aim, it was stressed, was for everyone to look as 'normal' as possible, otherwise what would be the point? This was not a beauty contest and upstaging the stars was definitely not on the agenda for any of us!

A catalogue to be made available to casting directors would include each individual's photograph together with accurate measurements, including height (in bare or stocking feet), hat and shoe size. Any radical changes in appearance, whether to do with hairstyle, weight gain or loss, visible piercings or tattoos were to be notified immediately to the agency. Body art in particular could severely limit an SA's options, especially in period dramas. In times gone by, tattoos were mainly associated with sailors and convicts and piercings, if any, kept firmly under wraps! (If Prince Albert really did have a 'Prince Albert', it was certainly never on public display.)

There was also space on the form to list any potentially useful hobbies or skills. Social dancing, for example, was a good one to have, and the ability to deliver silver service efficiently in a restaurant scene. (Napkin folding wasn't mentioned at the time, although I was once called upon to create a 'bishop's mitre' on camera. More of that later.)

Proficiency in a foreign language could also be useful. (One man I know, born in the former USSR, was promoted from the ranks during his first booking to bark out an order as a Russian security guard. Travel to Moscow wasn't part of the deal – the steps of his local town hall stood in for the entrance to the Kremlin - but he dined out on the experience for years.)

An hour later, it was all over. Undaunted but with my head in something of a spin, I returned home to wait for that all important phone call. It came a week later together with a very early call time in a coastal town forty miles away, directions to the unit base and a stern reminder to be punctual.

MY FIRST DAY AS AN SA

The following is lightly edited from my diary...

Up at half past four, I shared a lift with another member of the agency, which spared me the worry of having both to drive and navigate. The unit base occupies part of a car park overlooking the sea. Warned by the agency about the necessity to arrive punctually for our call time, we arrived well before seven o'clock to find the area bustling with people whose part in the proceedings it took me a long time to work out. All were casually dressed and, as befitted a sunny morning in early summer, most of the men wore baseball caps and long baggy shorts with plenty of pockets. Eventually we found an assistant director and were told to line up for some breakfast from the catering van and then report to the costume and makeup departments in their respective vans.

At that hour of the morning, I really wasn't hungry and made the mistake, never to be repeated, of settling for a just a cup of coffee. As I discovered from an experienced SA, days on set can be very long. The basic nine hours is just a starting point, and the timing of lunch depends very much on how the shoot is going. Two or even three o'clock in the afternoon isn't unheard of, so turning down a hearty breakfast is very unwise. She added that the caterers do wonders in the very limited space available to them and keep everyone very well fed from dawn till dusk. Sometimes well beyond.

Any illusions I might have had about glamour were swiftly dispelled as I donned the demure green suit, pale pink blouse and lace up shoes in the plastic bag with my name on it. The show, being set in the 1960s, is classed as period drama and ladies of my age are excluded from the more colourful outfits sported by the young of that time. We can, however, be in fashion from the neck upwards and I emerged from the makeup van with my hair backcombed and lacquered into a bouffant style that even the wind blowing off the sea would struggle to move. Eye liner, mascara and pink lipstick had also been lavishly applied and I hardly recognised myself in the mirror.

The day passed in a blur as I tried to get to grips with the novelty of it all. I was among a group of SAs taken off in a minibus to work inside a traditional town centre pub. The scene featured some very well known actors and I had to try not to gaze at them too obviously. Fortunately, a minor technical hiccup helped with this. There weren't enough smokers among us to generate an authentic atmosphere, so a machine was brought in to assist. It did so with such efficiency that we could hardly see across the bar at one point and one of the actors kept everyone in stitches with comments like "Where are you, Holmes?"

I was fascinated by other technical aspects, such as the sunshine and clouds seen through the windows but provided by crew outside the pub using special lights and cut outs. The beverages in our glasses were definitely non-alcoholic and the cigarette packets carefully sourced or reproduced to be right for the period.

At the end of the shoot, there was added drama outside the pub. While we were waiting for the minibus to take us back to the unit base, some likely lads tried to steal a box of props, thinking, no doubt, that the beer and cigarettes inside were the genuine article. Pursued by the police on duty to control the traffic, they didn't get far. Maybe that was a shame, as their street cred would have been severely dented if they'd tried to share the spoils with their friends. Not being required for any more scenes that day, we were 'cleared' around half past five. It took me nearly as long to disentangle my hair from all the back combing and lacquer as to travel back home! As for the eye makeup...

A few weeks went by before my next call...

III
HONESTY IS THE BEST POLICY

Generally speaking, all that was required of me as an SA was a professional attitude to the task in hand. This could be summed up as paying attention to what was required of me personally as well as the technical aspects and an understanding of what the scene was trying to convey.

There were, however, specialist casting agencies that recruited, for example, dancers, models, serving or former police officers, sports people and stunt performers.

Stunt artists trained for years to act as body doubles for the trickier manoeuvres. Falling or being pushed from an upstairs window, even with an unseen crash mat or pile of cardboard boxes to cushion the impact, was no guarantee against an awkward landing. Not to put too fine a point on it, those intrepid performers were replaceable, whereas a star's death or serious injury could mean a production's cancellation or postponement.

Claims to be able to drive, ride, ski, sing, tap dance or parachute, to name but a few skills, have to be genuine. It would be embarrassing, to say the least, and potentially dangerous to have your bluff called on the day.

I can only think of one SA who claimed to have got away with it. Keen to land a booking as an alien invader in a science fiction series, he'd assured his agent that he could ride. After all, he'd told himself, how hard could it be? Seaside donkeys had never given him any trouble and it was just a matter of scaling up. To be on the safe side, though, he did book a few lessons at a riding school during the week beforehand and was allocated a gentle old horse suitable for a beginner. Piece of cake! Or so he thought.

At the crack of dawn on the summer's day chosen for the shoot, he turned up full of confidence and was presented with an enormous black stallion. This was to be no leisurely hack either. He and his fellow alien invaders were expected to gallop along the long sandy beach against the incoming tide and had to do it in just one 'take'. Hanging on for dear life, he managed it – just – but had nightmares about it for months and swore never again to bite off more than he could comfortably chew.

With the best intentions in the world, though, it was still possible to be caught on the hop. Squeamish from childhood, I could never even bear to look at the specimens placed on my desk during biology exams, much less touch them, and I scraped though by memorising the illustrations in the textbooks. I'm also, purely by choice, a vegetarian.

Imagine my horror, then, when I was called upon one day to to join a line up of ladies plucking freshly killed pheasants! We were supposed to be applying for employment in a big country house and that was just one of the tasks set to assess our capabilities. Fortunately, as I hadn't been notified in advance that this would happen, no pressure was put upon me to do it and everyone laughed when I said that I'd rather run naked round the grounds. (In case you're wondering, they didn't take me up on it.) That, by the way, was the day that I was taught how to fold a bishop's mitre, as setting the table for a grand dinner was another of the skills we were required to demonstrate. (Some coaching from an expert went on before that scene.) We also had to arrange flowers, iron a shirt and choose a bottle of wine from the cellar, blowing off the (artificial) cobwebs. That day, which had started very badly for me, turned out to be a lot of fun.

IV
FINDING THE LOCATION
(AND PARKING WOES)

Getting to locations at the crack of dawn, or well beforehand at certain times of year, and in all weathers was one of the downsides of working as an SA. I was often surprised by how far some people were willing to travel for a single day's work, with their costs having the potential to outweigh any financial benefit. I made the decision right at the beginning only to accept bookings within the boundaries of Yorkshire, but it isn't known as 'the county of the broad acres' for nothing. There was still a lot of driving involved, almost always on my own.

Much of *Heartbeat*, for example, was filmed on the North Yorkshire Moors, but a former mill in Farsley housed its indoor sets. A building in Scarborough was used for the exterior of *The Royal*, although a Bradford hospital provided its interior. *Emmerdale* had large studios in Leeds but also a life size replica of Esholt, the village originally used, purpose built on the Harewood estate. All three shows also made use of many other locations, urban, rural and on the coast. *A Touch of Frost* included many scenes filmed around Wakefield and neighbouring small towns and so it went on. How I envied SAs able to split the cost by car sharing as well as giving each other companionship on the journey! With no railway station near my home and only limited bus services, public transport was rarely an option. I always calculated how long a journey should take and then gave myself at least an hour longer, two or more in foggy or very wintry conditions.

Even in good weather, road works that sprang up overnight like mushrooms or an accident could necessitate a long detour or even prompt the decision to park the car a good distance away and walk, either dragging a case on wheels or bowed under the weight of a holdall. For the record, I was never actually late, although I did once or twice make it by the skin of my teeth. Due to film at a garden centre on a very busy thoroughfare, I must have driven past it a dozen times before managing to spot a tiny sign set well back from the road. The star arrived by helicopter and was just landing as I parked my car. Far more often, I turned up embarrassingly early and had to twiddle my thumbs watching the crew set up their equipment.

SAs hailing from urban areas weren't always aware of limited transport services in the countryside. I remember one girl descending from her train and expecting to step straight onto a bus for the village, several miles away, where the shoot was to take place

"Next one's on Tuesday", she was told. The taxi she was then obliged to take wiped out much of her fee for the day. At least someone gave her a lift back to the station after we'd 'wrapped', but that must have been small consolation.

Directions issued in the early days could be quite sketchy.

"If you see the sea, you'll know you've missed the turning for the unit base," is one I remember particularly well. Another time, I found myself completely alone in a car park at six o'clock in the morning, the company having switched to another one close by and omitted to send out fresh information. Sent to take part in a commercial at a football stadium, I arrived in plenty of time but on the wrong side of a barrier with no way of getting through. On that occasion, I was saved by the location manager who, spotting my desperate signals, jumped into his car and drove round through heavy traffic to guide me to where I was supposed to be.

Where several little towns had been absorbed into large metropolitan areas, signs could be particularly misleading. Struggling to find my way through one urban sprawl, I was relieved to spot one pointing to the town centre, only to follow it for miles and find myself in the centre of the wrong town.

Although satellite navigation was generally a better option than relying on printed maps, it wasn't foolproof and I heard many horror stories from other SAs. Signals had been distorted by poor reception or obstructed by tall buildings or even trees. I never actually drove off a quayside, as one of them claimed to have done, but I was sometimes directed the wrong way down one-way streets and even once onto the slip road from a motorway.

As for parking, well, in an ideal world an SA would find ample free spaces laid on courtesy of the company. In my experience, sadly, this was rarely the case. When studio car parks were out of bounds for us, I had to lash out several pounds to 'pay and display' or take a chance on leaving my car wherever I could find a free spot. The first option, although generally safer, wasn't invariably so. I remember one SA returning after a long winter's day out on location to find that her car had disappeared. No one legally authorised, she was informed, was available to take a look at the CCTV footage and it was purely by luck that she got it back a week later, dumped but undamaged by the joy riders who'd taken it.

I never had a car stolen, probably because mine were (and still are) invariably elderly and on no one's wish list, but I did incur damage. One studio I went to several times had a patch of waste ground behind it on which anyone was allowed to park but, with no marked spaces, it was something of a free for all. One evening I came out to find that I had a bent and broken wing mirror and scratched and dented wing. My fee for that day didn't even come close to covering the repairs.

My one and only parking fine still rankles. The rules had changed since the previous occasion that I'd used that car park and I didn't have quite enough change for the new 'full day'. With no time to go off and find any more before I was due to sign in (and the machines hadn't then started to accept cards) I fed in the old amount and crossed my fingers. Luck wasn't on my side. Our kindly driver made a detour to drop off another SA at the railway station and, for the sake of that few minutes, I lost a substantial part of my fee for the day.

On a brighter note, once signed in, SAs were usually driven to other locations, sometimes sharing the vehicle with cast or crew members. After battling with the morning traffic and confusing road signs, it was good to sit back and relax while a professional driver familiar with the area took the wheel.

V
KNOWING ONE'S PLACE

There were certain 'deadly sins' to be avoided by SAs hoping to be rebooked. The list below isn't exhaustive, but it includes those I consider to be the most important.

- Missing your call time
- Arguing or trying to be too helpful
- Talking loudly and/or out of turn.
- Not biting your tongue when you disagree with an instruction
- Mobile going off on set
- Pestering the cast for selfies and other favours
- Taking photos on set
- Passing on spoilers or gossip to the media
- Barging to the front of the lunch queue
- Hogging the free refreshments

I only ever met one director who insisted that everyone on his set was equal. He'd been delayed in a meeting, but refused our offer to give way to him in the lunch queue. The irony was that one of the runners had just been reminding us about etiquette and the look on her face was priceless.

Generally speaking, there was a definite pecking order with

SAs firmly at the bottom. This was most evident at mealtimes and during breaks, when cast and crew took precedence. It wasn't just a status thing, although it could feel like that at busy times when we were hungry and so far back in the queue that we could hardly see the serving area. To be fair, the actors might have had lines to learn for their next scene and the crew responsibility for setting it up. Children (and their chaperones) were also served before adult SAs and I saw no problem with that. Being last was only really a problem for me on the odd occasion when no vegetarian options were left by the time I reached the front. (It did happen occasionally, though, that those of us who were still being served when everyone else had finished their food were called back onto the set before we'd had chance to digest ours.)

That said, major companies generally ensured that there was plenty to go round, although pickings could be slimmer if very large numbers were involved. I usually enjoyed a full English breakfast, two course lunch, evening meal if working very late and drinks and snacks at regular intervals during the day. The caterers, often operating from vans, did a remarkable job. A typical lunch for me could be cheese and onion pie with sautéed potatoes and fresh veg with a green sauce followed by a choice of rhubarb and gooseberry crumble with custard or a large wedge of chocolate cake with cream, fresh fruit and strawberries. They really pulled out the stops in the run up to Christmas and I enjoyed some magnificent lunches with all the trimmings.

The only time I remember patience being tested to the very limit was a summer when I was one of several dozen SAs booked for three days by an overseas film company. Not warned in advance to take a packed lunch, we only discovered on first arriving at the isolated location that no catering provision whatsoever had been made for us. There was nowhere in the vicinity to buy anything and, to make matters worse, trestle tables were groaning under the weight of an ample breakfast for everyone else. When one brave soul attempted to help herself to a cup of tea, she was shouted at and actually had her hand slapped down by a member of the crew. Mayhem ensued and it was only when people started phoning their equally appalled agents and a mass walkout was threatened that the director grudgingly agreed to allow us hot drinks straight away and send out for some snack food. As far as I recall, we got one sandwich each with no choice of filling, a small bag of crisps and a chocolate biscuit. Eking out these meagre rations, we gazed like Victorian street urchins at the lavish food laid on for everyone else. The other days were slightly better but not much. What we saw of the storyline looked very improbable and a cast member who'd been in very successful productions up to that point told some of us on our last afternoon that he hoped none of his friends would ever see the film. He probably got his wish, because it went straight to DVD and I've never yet met anyone who's even heard of it.

In studio canteens, some of which provided free meals and others not, we SAs sometimes had our own designated tables. Out on location, catering buses were provided. These were often old double deckers fitted out with tables and equipped with cutlery and condiments. A sign in the window directed us to the right one, which we generally had to ourselves. I do remember one day, though, when a famous singer who was guest starring on the show chose to have his lunch with us. A delightful man as well as a great performer, he offered photos and autographs to anyone who'd like them, things which SAs were strongly discouraged from ever requesting.

That was all part of being professional. While I wouldn't go as far as saying that we were expected to treat the cast like royalty, although some might, it was necessary to remember that no one liked to be pestered for favours in a work place situation. Actors appeared at their best or their worst at different times, but whatever happened, including conversations overheard, had to remain confidential. 'What happens on set, stays on set' was a good watchword to follow. It was also important to remain calm and collected even when others were not. Tempers were often frayed after a long day or a series of mishaps, but a slanging match benefited nobody and was unlikely to be forgiven or forgotten.

In my experience, most people were courteous and many were only too happy to chat during breaks. I've taken part in a fair few courtroom scenes over the years, both as a member of the jury and a spectator in the public gallery, and I particularly remember one very well known actress leaning over the side of the dock between takes to entertain everyone with risqué anecdotes. As soon as work resumed, though, the laughter stopped and she snapped straight back into her role as if her own life as well as that of her character were at stake.

I had some very enjoyable conversations about common interests and, especially with older actors, insights into films and TV programmes that I'd loved over the years. Although long past being star struck, I still had to pinch myself sometimes to believe that I was actually chatting to someone who'd played a major role in a Hammer Horror film that had frightened the living daylights out of me as a teenager. He even told me how some of the special effects were done, which was quite a revelation. An actor who'd had my whole family rocking with mirth on the radio and then as part of the *Carry On* team was still going strong way past the age at which most would have retired, and he hadn't changed a bit.

It was interesting to see how some of the people I was privileged to meet in real life were very much like the characters for which they were best known, while others were completely different. I bonded immediately with one lady over our mutual love of cats and another told me that she only ever read the parts of a script in which she was involved, because she liked to watch the show as a 'punter'. Several mentioned coming up the hard way through rep and lamented the fact that youngsters fresh out of drama school would miss out on that experience.

Especially fascinating to meet were actors who'd avoided being stereotyped and gone from medieval hero to 21st century villain, plain Jane to femme fatale, no-hoper to captain of industry or vice versa and slipped without apparent effort into the right look and voice for each part. Long a fan of *Doctor Who*, I was gripped by a tale told by a gentleman usually cast as a smooth upper crust character about his appearance in that show as a grotesque alien. Another time, I worked with someone whose father had actually been one of the Doctors and I even met the mother-in-law of a villain from *The Lord of the Rings*! An actor best known for his role as a top civil servant but playing the part of a wily butler when I met him kept us all entertained during one lunch break with a whole string of unrepeatable jokes.

Not all child actors continue in show business and not all actors begin as children, but it was particularly interesting to follow the career progression of those who did. Some remained with the same series, but most took on fresh challenges, including taking part in popular reality shows.

The only downside to spending time with well known faces of

all ages was that it sometimes had a negative impact on my enjoyment of their performances in other roles. Remembering the time someone proudly showed me a photo of his new kitchen or shared worries about a child's first day at school, made seeing him as a contract killer or medieval warlord quite a stretch! As a fan of American fantasy horror, I was very taken with a devastatingly attractive vampire on one particular series until I realised that we'd actually worked together once. If only he'd looked like that then! The fangs made all the difference!

I suppose mixing with so many actors and SAs has given me a stronger stomach for watching violence on screen. Having heard their (often hilarious) stories about how the scenes were shot and witnessed some myself, I'm now mostly unmoved by blood and gore rather than covering my eyes with a cushion as I used to.

As for sex scenes, well...

VI
ALWAYS MORE TO LEARN

I was always coming across new words and phrases, but some of the most common were these:

ACTION: The scene begins here. Some people will move immediately. Others will wait for a few 'beats' and may go, for example, on Action + 5, for easier timing.

BLOCKING: The movements of everyone within a scene

CALL TIME: The time for each individual actor to be ready to start work, as listed on their call sheet

CONTINUITY: Ensuring that details remain the same during multiple shots. Frequent photographs are taken of the set and everyone involved. Someone seen walking into a pub and then appearing in the bar, for example, must appear exactly the same, even if the shots were taken in different locations and on different days.

CUT: Stop! The scene may be complete, or need resetting.

DINING BUS: An old bus fitted out with tables, cutlery etc.

DOLLY: A track for the camera operator to move along

DOING A BANANA: Curving round on a specific path, instead of walking in a straight line

DOUGAL: A furry microphone cover, named after the character from The Magic Roundabout

FIRST POSITIONS: Where everyone is at the start of a scene

HONEY WAGONS: Portable toilets

JELLY BABY: A fake (usually very realistic looking) infant

PICK UP: Refilming part of a scene from a specific point

RESET: Back to first positions

ROLLING: Action is about to begin as the cameras (and/or sound) are rolling to film a take. It's also a signal to pay close attention and be quiet.

RUNNER: An entry-level position. Gives assistance wherever required.

SET: Wherever the action is taking place

STAND BY: Be prepared for rolling

TAKE: Actual filming when a scene has been rehearsed

TURN OVER: Time for Sound and Cameras to roll

WILD TRACK: A general hubbub recorded on set for use as background noise. Added during the editing process.

WRAP: The director is satisfied, and the shoot is finished.

It was also a good idea to learn the names of the actors as well as the characters they played, the former being more commonly used on set. I also learned a few nicknames but trod very carefully, not wishing to attempt a level of camaraderie that might not have been acceptable.

Knowing who was who on one of my first few days on set would have saved me considerable embarrassment. Told to go and stand next to 'Amy' I had no idea who that was and floundered until a friendly voice called out, "I'm Amy, actually," and there was a gale of laughter. She was one of the stars of the show and it was lucky for me that she was amused rather than offended. After that, I took great pains with my research.

When someone had moved from a long established role in a popular series to a completely different one, it could be quite difficult not to slip up and I've nearly bitten my tongue off once or twice. Queuing up for breakfast on a dismal British morning behind someone previously only seen in a sun-drenched Australian soap was quite an experience, as was having an actor who'd chilled my blood in a crime drama asking if I had change for a vending machine. Once in a while, a character 'changed heads', meaning that a different actor took over the role, which could be particularly disconcerting.

On most productions there were far more people behind the camera than in front of it. Most of those I met were happy to be on first name terms, but I never just assumed that they would be. The people in charge of SAs were usually 3rd assistant directors (ADs) and they signed us in, made sure that we were where we needed to be at all times and signed us out when we were 'cleared'. A 1st or 2nd AD generally told us what to do when we were actually on set, although those instructions were often passed on through the 3rd AD or even a runner. We rarely saw the director, who spent most of his/her time monitoring what went on from behind the scenes.

It was easy to pick out the people in charge of cameras and sound, but other crew members milling around purposefully with radios, headphones, clipboards, tool kits and all sorts of other equipment were harder to identify. No one wore a badge, which would have been very helpful, and I never did quite work out what some of them did.

VII
LOOKING THE PART

Here's another extract from my diary.

> *Awful weather, so I rang to check that the shoot was still on. It was. Call time 2.30. Drove to the base camp and was given my tasteful costume – a brown and orange floral dress, well above the knees, high heeled brown shoes, tan tights and a whitish duster coat. I was also issued with a frumpy brown handbag and ancient suitcase. There were no curtains on the changing hut, so I was glad to be in sensible underwear. An SA I'd never met before refused to have a trim on the grounds that he wouldn't have had short hair in the 1960s.*
>
> *"Ah, but your father would have," was the rejoinder from the costume lady. What a put down!*

Depending on the requirements of the production to which I was sent, I was either given a set of clothes, sometimes a uniform, to wear or asked to take along a selection from my own wardrobe. In the latter case, I'd have been briefed on what was appropriate for the season in which the action was to be set and my part in it.

Even when I was expecting only to take part in a single scene or episode of a drama, I got into the habit of taking at least three outfits for Costume to choose from. Separates worked well, although on one occasion I was asked to wear a white blouse and floral skirt that were never intended to go together. That just had to be the day that I appeared prominently behind the opening titles of the show!

Care was usually taken to ensure an assortment of colours, but I remember a group of us once being told we were fine as we were for the first episode and could please ourselves for the second. That backfired later on, when everyone wore dark blue, but I think the director must have been in a hurry, because he let it go.

It was particularly important that an SA's outfit didn't coincide, clash with or draw the viewers' eyes away from whatever a member of the cast was wearing. In addition, garments with logos were definitely out. Reds, checks and stripes too, because they could make the cameras 'flare'.

Sparkly clothes weren't usually a good idea either. I tended to pack neutral colours with no distracting patterns – a plain grey jacket with a light pastel blouse, for example – and, unless told otherwise in advance, avoided wearing too much white, black or conspicuous jewellery. Shoes were also something to think about. To avoid clip-clopping across a set, I learned to choose soft soles. The alternative was to walk more or less on my toes, which looked and felt very strange. Even with the best intentions in the world, however, I didn't always get it right, as in this diary entry:

> *The Wardrobe lady lamented the fact that I wasn't suitably dressed for late September/early October and made me wear a pale blue Dannimac to sit outside the café in blazing sunshine pretending to eat a prop muffin and piece of cheesecake – both wooden or plaster!*

Things sometimes went wrong due to a message going astray, a last minute change of plan or a sudden deterioration in the weather. One episode that comes to mind was a continuity nightmare with the first guests to arrive at a church wedding flushed and fanning themselves from the heat while the last had snow on their shoulders.

'Smart' meant different things to different people. I remember a two-day shoot involving dozens of SAs from different agencies that saw some of us arriving dressed for shopping in the high street and others as though bound for Royal Ascot. All supposed to be guests at the same function, we must have been an odd sight. There was nothing to be done, though. The location, not a cheap one, had been booked and, for continuity, we had to wear exactly the same outfits on the second day.

There had obviously been a breakdown in communication when a large group of SAs turned up on time only to be asked to change into their pyjamas. This was the first that anyone had heard of that requirement and the company involved had to scour nearby shops for enough cheap sets to go round. Filming was delayed for a couple of hours, but that was considered better than cancelling the shoot altogether.

Wearing my own clothes for contemporary dramas was fine in terms of fit but often uncomfortable for the season in which the action was set. A balmy day in late October, for example, might have seen me swathed in a winter coat, woolly hat, thick scarf and sheepskin boots. A chilly late spring might have called for beachwear. Comfortable dressing rooms with full length mirrors and plenty of hanging space would have been wonderful, but I often had to squeeze into a small portable cabin with a dozen other SAs, change in the Ladies or even resort to a dark corner somewhere behind the set. On one occasion, a movable clothes rack provided the only privacy in a very large hall and SAs of different genders had to take turns behind it. Although not troubled by excessive modesty, I was once again pleased not to have worn skimpy underwear!

Regular SAs did amass a collection of clothes for every occasion, albeit often sourced in charity shops, but it was a blessèd relief to be offered a uniformed part. Always assuming, of course that the uniform was a good fit!

Taking part in a 'period drama', whether set well within living memory or in the Dark Ages, involved being kitted out from head to toe. Waistbands that felt snug first thing in the morning became increasingly uncomfortable as the day went on and were sometimes sawing me in half by the time I was cleared. My worst experience was having to wear a ridiculously tight 'pencil' skirt with no lining to the pockets. It split during lunch and a harassed costume lady had to sew me back into it for the remaining scenes. For obvious reasons, not a drop of liquid passed my lips for the rest of the day.

Corsets, knee-length breeches – only to be donned by a gentleman once his stockings were firmly in place, or so I was told – garters and so on all left their mark and some scenes really tested the footwear handed out at the beginning of the day. Although everyone's size was on record and generally adhered to, the shoes provided could be narrow fitting or have heels too high for a lot of walking about to be comfortable. Stiletto-heeled 'winkle pickers' left me with an impressive array of blisters one day, but it could have been worse. Another SA complained all morning of itchy ankles and swore that the boots she'd been given to wear were infested with fleas. She had the bites to prove it when she took them off.

Some people fell in love with their costumes, though, and just had to have a photo taken. I remember one chap covering himself with glory when he struck a pose inside the male SAs' caravan and put the horns of his helmet straight through the ceiling. It didn't help his case that the 'warriors' had been specifically told to leave their headgear outside during the breaks.

Being short-sighted from childhood gave me other considerations to deal with. My usual specs were fine for most scenes set in the present day, unless I was standing or seated in such a position that they reflected the studio lights. (There was sometimes a similar situation outdoors with the sunshine and my prescription dark glasses, in which case I was politely asked to take them off) For period dramas, though, the frames were hopelessly wrong. I had to resort to contact lenses, although they also had drawbacks (and I don't just mean dropping them down the plughole, putting them in the wrong eyes or getting them stuck, although I've done all those things.) My lenses were fine for distance but no good at all for print. On one occasion, I just stared hopelessly when offered a copy of the script in order to see the line a character was going to speak before I had to move from A to B. Another day, I couldn't make out what was on the lunch menu. Another SA was reading it out to me when one of the cast took over and I've often wondered whether the tale went around that I was illiterate. After that, I tried to remember to take along a pair of reading glasses but often forgot to swap them from one outfit to another.

I particularly regretted that when I spent almost a whole day in a hospital bed with a pile of glossy magazines that I was unable to read. Instructed to ignore the scenes being played out around me, I just had to stare at the blurry pages and try to look absorbed in them. The only consolation was that the star in the next bed had 'visitors' who brought real chocolates and she was very generous with them between takes. Lovely lady!

By the way, a general rule with magazines used on set was that titles should be hidden – something to do with product placement rules. In any case, they were generally very out of date and I actually found one article that I'd written and quite forgotten about. I remember an actor once telling me that that he'd seen the magazine that I was pretending to read when he'd been starring in another show six years previously. Newspapers, on the other hand, at least the covers, were often printed especially to tie in with whatever was supposed to be going on.

Making up my face in the morning, I generally went for a light touch that was easy to remove or add to as required. Expecting to be a hospital visitor, I once arrived to find myself ordered to scrub off every bit of makeup and prepare to spend the day in bed as a very poorly patient. That kind of sudden change, not uncommon, wasn't always welcome. I remember someone booked as a body double for one of the cast, which paid considerably more than our basic rate, being told when he arrived that he'd just be working as an SA. He was most displeased and let everyone know it.

I always enjoyed being summoned into the makeup van for the full works. Series set in the 1960s required heavy eye liner and bouffant hair. The eye liner, generally black, had 'wings'. The bouffant was created by energetic back combing and held in place with generous amounts of hair spray. A French pleat or chignon also required large numbers of hairpins. On wet or windy days, old fashioned plastic rain hoods were handed out to cover the creation until the very last moment.

Men didn't escape scrutiny, of course. Depending on the period, they might be given appropriate haircuts or have false sideburns attached, which they were required to hand in at the end of the day. Bald heads were frequently powdered to prevent unwanted shine.

On set, makeup artists and trainees with huge see-through plastic shoulder bags full of cosmetics and hair-styling equipment were constantly on standby. Their main focus, of course, was on cast members, every aspect of whose appearance was tweaked before a take, but not doing the same for SAs could lead to some strange anomalies. On one particularly windy day, I was summoned indoors at the last moment and placed next to one of the leading actors in a scene. On screen, I looked as though I'd been blown through a hedge. He didn't have a hair out of place.

An aspect of the makeup team's work that I particularly admired was the ability to create fake injuries in the aftermath of accidents or fight scenes. I once saw an actor having terrible trouble when the tissue he was holding up to his nose kept getting stuck onto the fake blood, but most of the transformations I saw were very convincing, even in close-up. A great deal of effort went into ensuring authenticity and one of my favourite memories is of an excessively sweaty and malodorous character having ever more moisture added to the underarms of his shirt to stop them drying out.

VIII

IT WASN'T ACTING, BUT…

Some SAs I met were also, had been or hoped to be actors, but those with professional training were a small minority. Most of us, who came from a very wide variety of backgrounds, just picked up what we needed to do on the job. A willingness to listen and do exactly what was asked were the main requirements.

Standing or seated in one spot throughout a scene, I'd be told whether or not to react to whatever was going on around me. If with other SAs, I'd probably be pretending to have a conversation. When alone, I might have been given something to read or be told to fiddle my phone. Switched off, of course!

As often as not, though, some movement would be required and the instructions could be quite complicated. From a given spot, of which I had to take careful note in order to return to it for subsequent rehearsals and takes, I used to follow the route prescribed. It might have been as simple as walking from one end of the set to the other, but often there was more to it than that. I also had to remember whether to set off on Action, slightly before, a few 'beats' afterwards or wait until a cast member did something or said a particular line. This would be typical:

> *On Action + 5, walk across to the shop. Look through the sale goods on display outside until you hear the police car approaching and then turn round and stare while it pulls up outside the doctor's. Nudge each other when he's brought out in handcuffs and wait until the police car moves off again. Go into the shop.*

I often had to repeat that sort of thing many times, depending on the number of hitches, camera angles required and so on and could walk miles up and down the same stretch of pavement. (An unfailingly gallant actor once told me that I'd 'crossed his path quite splendidly on every occasion'.) Getting even the shortest scene done in one take was very rare indeed. While something messy involving a JCB was going on behind me, I once strolled over to a post box fourteen times before we were done. (It was lucky that a member of the props department had brought along a whole stack of identical letters for me.) Something that would take less than a minute of screen time and might be cut altogether could easily take an hour or longer. Learning that gave me an insight into why productions were so expensive to make. That and the sheer number of people involved.

Whether taking part in an indoor or outdoor scene, I always had to assume that I was in shot unless specifically told otherwise. It wasn't always easy to see where the cameras were pointing or to know how wide the lenses were! A surreptitious scratch or worse might well be captured for posterity! On a purpose built studio set, walls could come and go and a camera might have been looking down on me from where the ceiling was supposed to be. Moving from room to room through one of those set ups always put me in mind of a visit to IKEA.

One scene I remember seemed to take forever to do and was made worse by the fact that, just as it seemed that nothing else could possibly go wrong, someone noticed that it was dark outside one window and broad daylight outside the other. We had to start all over again.

IX
SOUND EFFECTS

While filming in outdoor locations, we often had to wait for aircraft to pass overhead and even rumbles of thunder could cause a delay. Indoors, apart from a ring tone from a phone (whose red-faced owner hastily switched it off) or a badly timed cough, things generally ran more smoothly. When I started out, whispering to each other during pretend conversations was fine and we used to play all kinds of word games, hoping that no lip readers were among the viewers.

"Aston Villa," I might say to another SA, to which he would respond, "Birmingham City" or "Bristol Rovers" and so on until we got to the end of the alphabet, ran out of inspiration or the scene finished. Later on, though, microphones became too sensitive for that, so we had to mime instead. It was harder to do, as we had nothing meaningful to react to. The temptation was for those with their backs to the camera just to let the others get on with it, only moving occasionally to avoid looking like cardboard cut outs.

In pub scenes, glasses and bottles had to be put down soundlessly, anyone arriving or leaving had to avoid their footwear click-clacking and solitary drinkers were told to avoid rustling their newspapers. I was once asked by a sound man not to crunch the crisps I'd been given to eat as part of the scene and had to suck my way through a whole packet of cheese and onion.

Any background noise required might be done by means of a 'wild track' filmed at the end, where everyone was asked to speak at once while watching one of the ADs raising and lowering a hand to indicate the level of sound required.

When required to sing, as part of a church congregation, for example, I used to mouth the words without producing much in the way of volume. (People who've heard me sing would understand why. I do know my limitations.) Cheering and chanting at a 'World Cup Final' was a different matter and I was quite hoarse by the end of the day. It was for a beer commercial never shown in this country, so I don't know how it turned out, but a hundred or so of us had to keep moving around to represent a crowd of thousands. No doubt skillful editing was employed to make it look convincing.

I didn't do many commercials, but they could be quite lucrative, especially for people given enough of a part to qualify for repeat fees.

X
EATING AND DRINKING AS PART OF THE ACTION

Many scenes I was in involved food, whether fake or real. Anything displayed in a shop window or on a counter was likely to be fake, but that served up to the cast and SAs at least usually started off as edible. Whether it remained so, depended on how long drawn out the scene turned out to be. The props department would usually be on standby to replace drinks and dishes as often as required. No one wanted a viewer to spot a cup of coffee with a skin on it!

In order for beer to have an authentic looking 'head', it needed to be real and warnings were given to drink it only during takes. Most 'alcoholic' drinks, though, were anything but. White or red grape juice often stood in for wine, a 'vodka shot' was likely to be plain water and fancy 'cocktails' might even contain jelly to make them look the part.

I've never forgotten the first time I was called upon to eat a scone on set. It looked quite fresh when it was put down in front of me and I cut it into bite-size pieces, only to have to reassemble it for each new take. I never did get to eat any of them and by the time we'd finished the scene they could have been used for ammunition.

What was placed in front of me in restaurant scenes was very much the luck of the draw. A salad was fine and I was happy to nibble the odd leaf, but some other offerings were never going to pass my lips. While other SAs were enjoying every mouthful of sausage and mash or fish and chips, for example, I was usually picking up and putting down the same forkful or just shuffling everything around on my plate.

Once signed in, I was obliged to stay until cleared, however late that was. Looking back, I think the longest 'day' I ever put in was around fourteen hours (not including driving to and from the location) and the shortest around an hour and a half. I was once left open-mouthed when my dinner partner looked at his watch and announced that he'd been double-booked and was due elsewhere. He dashed off, leaving me chatting animatedly into the air. The director was furious and I'd be very surprised if the man ever reappeared in that particular show.

My happiest 'food' memory is of the time a whole restaurant had been taken over for the evening. The owner was a great fan of that particular show and invited the SAs as well as the cast to choose anything they fancied from his extensive menu. There were some delicious vegetarian options and I didn't waste a mouthful. On the other hand, I was unfortunate to be present when a young actor was given a choice of three different types of soup to 'vomit up' after a night on the tiles. Not a pretty sight!

XI
MIXED MESSAGES

Unlike cast members, who often put forward their own suggestions, SAs were expected to do exactly as they were told without question. Usually the task was quite clear, but occasionally conflicting instructions could cause confusion and then the question arose as to whom to obey. Remember that an SA was outranked even by a child actor, much as a 19th century sailor was subordinate to a twelve-year-old midshipman, and some, with years of experience behind them, had very decided opinions about how things should be done.

Very, very occasionally, an SA might receive an instruction from the director in person. That was known as 'being given a note' and would be challenged by no one! In all the years I worked in television and film, it only happened to me once and I cherished the moment.

I once found myself in a dilemma when a veteran actor to whom I was supposed to give the briefest nod of recognition as our paths crossed at a busy social gathering insisted that I hold out my hand for him to shake. Poo-pooing my hesitation, he then turned down my muttered suggestion that maybe he should offer me his hand instead, which – leaving me with no option but to take it – would have exonerated me from any blame. He'd been brought up, he then said, to believe that a lady should always offer her hand to a gentleman and not the other way round. In the end, I did as he wished and heaved a sigh of relief when no one seemed to notice.

My trepidation then may have been fuelled by the fact that

there had already been a kerfuffle earlier that day. A group of us had been obliged by cast members getting in the way to deviate from the route prescribed for our walk across the large outdoor set. Standing at the wrong angle to see why we'd done this, the 2nd AD really let fly but did at least have the grace to apologise later when one of the runners explained what had happened. How much worse would it have been, I wondered later, if we'd just stuck to our instructions, elbowing the actors aside.

A solo walk for me down a steep street at twilight ended very abruptly when I spotted thick electric cables snaking across the pavement. "You could just jump over them," suggested one of the cast, but I certainly didn't. With all the technical wizardry involved in shooting a scene, trips and falls over equipment were an ever present possibility, especially in poor lighting conditions. We reset and I did a banana!

XII
WORKING WITH CHILDREN

Looking back, I can honestly say that I never saw a child treated with anything but the utmost care and consideration. It was all a far cry from the horror stories still told about the early days of Hollywood, where young stars, seen as mere commodities by some studios, were open to every kind of abuse and exploitation.

Before acquiring this knowledge, though, I was shocked to the core by something I saw during my first time on a hospital set. As soon as tea was announced, a young woman who'd been crooning lovingly to the baby in her arms seized it by one ankle and tossed it over to one of the crew.

"About time too!" she said with a sigh of relief. "I'm parched." Seeing my stunned expression, the man who'd caught the unfortunate infant brought it over to me and said with an amused grin on his face, "It's only a jelly baby, you know."

Weighing the same as a newborn, its delicate features made the silicone version so lifelike that I found myself holding it just like a real baby. One of those turned up later, accompanied by its mother and a licensed chaperone, and was on set for a very short time for a few close ups before being whisked away for a feed and nappy change. (When a birth was written into a storyline, as I discovered later, a call generally went out to casting agents to approach new or even expectant parents and a baby would be chosen from a shortlist.)

Sometimes I saw identical twins far too young to take direction sharing a role, which could double the time a real baby was allowed in front of the camera. It was also useful when one baby fell asleep or was having an 'off day'. In any case, the infants all had their own personalities, with some usually better at sitting quietly with their toys and others at interacting with those around them. They weren't in the least impressed by fame, of course, and sometimes both the child and the actor holding it had to be hastily cleaned up.

I was reminded of the twin sisters who played Carrie Ingalls in *The Little House on the Prairie.* Their first names were curiously run together in the credits as Lindsay Sidney Greenbush and it was years before I realised that Lindsay and Sidney were in fact two girls.

I was often struck by the professionalism of older children, who usually seemed to enjoy what they were required to do. On the rare occasion that someone was uncooperative, the approach was definitely 'carrot' (more likely mini marshmallows) rather than 'stick'. In between their scenes and still under the watchful gaze of the chaperones (legally required for all under-16s), they also had a lot of fun. It was generally understood that they were never to be exposed to secondary smoking or bad language, but joining in with impromptu kickabouts and other games was fine.

Towards the end of my time as an SA a requirement was brought in for everyone to go through regular DBS checks. While regretting the necessity, I accepted that every walk of life had its bad apples and the children's safety was paramount.

XIII

ANIMAL ENCOUNTERS

'No animals were harmed during the making of this programme' often appears in end credits. Whether that is always true, I'm not in a position to say, but certainly all those I've been around on set have been well treated. Owners and handlers generally displayed the same amount of vigilance as the children's chaperones mentioned in the previous chapter.

Actors whose characters were identified with a particular pet became very fond of them. I remember one scene being held up for ages because a little dog refused to sit up on its mistress's knee and bribery certainly provided the solution that day.

A great deal of trouble was taken not to put an animal under stress and part of that, as with the human twins, was often to provide a matching pair. I was once supplied with two very lively chihuahuas to be carried under my arm in strict rotation. As the afternoon wore on, rehearsals were followed by flawed takes, mainly due to technical hitches, and both little dogs started to fret. To everyone's amusement, they were then replaced with a wooden cut out of a blue rhino for me to carry around until their owner thought it time for one of them to be picked up again. Quite right too!

Never a dog owner myself, I found being allocated one to 'walk' quite a challenging experience on another day, but that was nothing compared to being cast one summer as a competition judge. As part of a large event, the 'dog show' was to be filmed over four consecutive and very long days. Continuity demanded that I wore the same outfit throughout, so it was completely filthy and covered in dog hairs by the end. Not only that, but the sun blazed down throughout and my face was boiled-lobster red. It was fun, though, with the dogs ranging from the tiniest chihuahua – again – to an enormous and very slobbery St Bernard. I fell in love with them all and would have awarded each and every one a rosette, had it really been my job to judge.

On outdoor sets there was always the possibility of wildlife putting in an unscheduled appearance. Sea gulls squawking overhead or dive bombing anyone with food were a nuisance, but everyone loved the hedgehogs who occasionally found their way into the cabins and the cheeky robins looking for crumbs after (or sometimes during) tea breaks. The much larger birds, determined to defend their patch, who attacked the helium balloons launched one morning to celebrate a character's birthday were less popular, at least with the director. I imagine it took him quite a while to see the funny side of that.

XIV

THRILLS AND SPILLS

Accidents and fights written into the script were carefully choreographed, with paramedics on hand in case they went wrong. If deemed too dangerous even for professional stunt performers, dummies were used to stand in for the actors. I remember once hearing a young SA say, "I could have done that," as a motorbike and rider hurtled over a cliff edge a few yards away from us. I thought that he was joking, but he was actually training hard in his spare time and did go on to be a stuntman.

I was close by when rivals for the same man's affections went at it hammer and tongs, albeit in slow motion to begin with. Each lady had been given a wig to wear with pieces that would pull out easily and on screen the fight looked very convincing.

All the same, mishaps could and did happen, such as someone forgetting to clear a table of glasses before an actor 'punched across the room' fell back onto it. I once saw a stunt performer who'd landed awkwardly after a fall from an upstairs window being taken away by emergency ambulance, not the one already in place for a dramatic end to the scene. It transpired that he'd badly injured his back and faced a lengthy spell in hospital.

Actors, I found, could be very tough. I remember one who was unwell but soldiered on with a sick bucket close at hand. He had a lot to contend with that day, because the little ones playing his grandchildren wouldn't co-operate and had to be replaced with dolls. I was also present when someone was nearly knocked out. A car door closed a couple of seconds too early by another member of the cast had caught her a hard blow on the side of the head and it was touch and go whether she could continue with the scene. She did, though, refusing to make a fuss despite 'the mother and father of all headaches'.

I count myself lucky never to have had to claim on my Equity insurance, but I came close a few times and never regretted paying the annual subscription. During a funeral scene one hot sunny day, after a very early start and next to no breakfast, I found myself lying flat on my back on a grassy slope. Opening my eyes to look up at the circle of worried faces, I wasn't sure whether I'd passed out or just taken a step backwards and lost my balance. One of the cast was holding my hand and another, wondering whether I might be diabetic (I'm not), was offering to get me a biscuit or some sugar.

Fortunately no real harm was done except to my pride and, despite my having held up filming, I couldn't fault the care taken to make sure that I was all right. Despite my insistence that I could carry on, a taxi was summoned at the company's expense to take me home in style. (The only downside to that was my dear husband having to take a long journey by public transport to retrieve my car from where I'd parked it by the studios, but he didn't mind.) Other SAs told me later that everyone had been asking about me. As a very small cog in the wheel of the show, I was agreeably surprised by their concern, which continued when I was back on set the following week.

Another incident occurred when I was filming out in the wilds and required to clamber in and out of the back of a lorry several times. It had been pouring down, the whole area was slippery and only the hastily offered helping hand of the lead actor saved me from falling several feet onto the road. The climax of that scene, incidentally, was when that same lorry was pushed over a cliff.

Intended to break up, it landed on its wheels, shot down the slope and almost took out one of the cameramen. I can still see the look of horror on his face as it hurtled towards him.

It wasn't always possible to see or hear what was happening on set and I remember once being told to leave a building a few beats after 'Action'. I was keeping my ear to the door when a runner hurtled in with fresh instructions and nearly knocked me for six.

Only on one occasion did I actually turn up for work when maybe I shouldn't have. A fall in the garden had left me with a sprained ankle, which was quite painful, but I didn't want to cancel at short notice. Everyone was very kind and one of the cast took great pains to find me a seat whenever possible. Method acting, perhaps? He was playing the part of a parish priest!

XV
PROPS AND PRACTICAL JOKES

All kinds of things were used to add reality to a scene and great care was taken to make them look fit for purpose. Shopping bags and suitcases, for example, were sometimes weighted to make sure that they were carried as if full and heavy.

Cast one day as a domestic servant in a grand house, my task was to wash a ground floor window whilst police enquiries were being pursued close by. It was a very windy day and whoever had prepared my bucket had been more than generous with the soap. The result was that suds flew all over the place, including into the eyes of a young constable, who didn't appreciate that one bit. Neither did the AD in charge of the scene, who had to call a halt to filming until my bucket had been emptied and refilled.

Goods 'for sale' tended to be a mixture of genuine and fake. A fellow SA and I were once instructed to browse the Christmas trees outside a shop, pick one up and take it to the far end of the large outdoor set. If only it had been plastic! It was large, very awkward to carry and there were many rehearsals and takes before that scene was complete. I should add, though, that my partner that day was a true gentleman, insisting on taking most of the weight of the wretched thing and quite exhausted by the time we were done.

Outdoor shoots relied a lot on the goodwill and co-operation of the public, most of whom didn't mind a little inconvenience and were happy to wait for permission to cross the set, but there were generally one or two who stood on their rights with regard to what was, after all, often a public thoroughfare. This was particularly true when there were no police on duty and harassed members of the crew were in charge of crowd control. One morning when the action was centred around an ice cream van, the SA inside was repeatedly harassed by a man wanting to buy a '99. He'd seen cornets being handed out in multiple takes to one of the actors and didn't see why he couldn't have one too. The poor SA, who only had a small tub of ice cream and no chocolate flakes, didn't know what to do, an AD hastened over to see what was going on and filming was held up for quite a while. Diplomacy prevailed in the end, although what shape it took I can't remember. At least we were able to carry on. The actor in receipt of all the cornets couldn't face another one by that time and started handing them out to all and sundry once out of shot.

Filming in front of an impromptu audience did have its amusing side. Even we SAs were occasionally asked for autographs, even if the eager fans must sometimes have wondered afterwards who on earth we were. Our names were never included in cast lists, although my face did appear a couple of times in TV magazines. Once it was very clear. The second time, I was bisected by the stem of a rose held by an actress in the foreground. At least I knew it was me by the hat I was wearing.

The most time I remember seeing wasted over a prop was in what we'd been promised would be the last scene before lunch. A child's toy, whether faulty or just overused I don't know, broke down every time it was activated. While it was being fixed for the umpteenth time, stomachs were starting to rumble and tempers to fray. My own job was to walk past the child with an indulgent smile on my face, but my jaw was aching by the time the director was satisfied.

Some props came with orders that they mustn't be touched by

any unauthorised person – that toy may have been one of those – but even quite ordinary looking furniture could be off limits, at least to SAs. Seats were sometimes in short supply for those of us waiting behind the scenes to be called onto the set and I remember someone once being turfed off a comfortable armchair on the grounds that it was part of a room set. Although diplomatically responding with a sweet smile and humble apology, she did wonder privately to the rest of us later on what possible harm she could have done to the chair by sitting on it for a few minutes. That contrasted sharply with what I saw on another show when the star, spotting SAs standing around awkwardly, refused to carry on until seats were found for us all.

A lot of larking around went on, particularly when things were otherwise rather slow. A crew member on one series was notorious for playing practical jokes on the eager and gullible. On one occasion, when a few of us were lining up with our suitcases to emerge one by one from a railway station, he said that the director had asked for someone to limp. A flurry of hands went up and the young man he chose did a good imitation of Herr Flick from *'Allo 'Allo!* The poor chap was mortified when asked what on earth he was playing at, by which time, of course, the prankster had disappeared.

An actor well known for his impish sense of humour once put me on the spot. My orders were to open the door of my home when he knocked, shake my head regretfully when he asked if I recognised the man in the photograph he was holding out to me and then close the door. We did this several times in rehearsal, but during the first take he threw me completely by whispering,

"That's not what you said last time." His back was to the camera and so he just grinned while I floundered. I suppose for a few seconds I must have looked like a rabbit caught in the headlights. Fortunately, the first take is rarely the one that's used and he didn't do it again.

XVI
OUT IN ALL SEASONS AND WEATHERS

The only aspect of my work as an SA that I shared with a fashion model was shooting so far ahead that the seasons were sometimes reversed. The hottest day of the year might see me sweltered in a thick winter coat and the coldest, after a long drive in the dark with the car's heater going full blast, shivering by the sea in a flimsy summer dress. I think I may have come close to hypothermia on some occasions and heat exhaustion on others, although most production teams did their best to take care of everyone. I remember SAs being given hand warmers to clutch when out in the snow. Without those, I doubt whether we'd have been able to hold a pen when it came time to sign out at the end of the day. Ice creams were sometimes supplied to keep us going during a heat wave, which was a very welcome treat.

Sadly, such consideration wasn't always the case and I remember looking on enviously when puffer jackets and umbrellas were produced for cast members between takes while SAs had to stand around soaking wet and shivering for long periods of time. I never put myself forward for a night shoot in winter but have heard horror stories from SAs who did. There was always the prospect of finding that the hot food had run out by the time they reached the front of the queue or that there was no real shelter from the elements in a rain-sodden field.

Generally speaking, agents were briefed on the type of clothing required, but liaison did sometimes break down and no one could ever guarantee the weather. Most people understood this, of course, although I did once witness a tantrum from an overseas director who'd gone to a lot of trouble to book a beauty spot for a picnic scene.

"It's August, for goodness' sake!" he kept shouting to anyone who'd listen. "It isn't supposed to rain."

Thermal underwear was a sensible investment in the colder months. (An older actress who'd played the same part for many years once confided in me that she'd love to wear thermal long johns and deeply regretted having insisted at the start that her character would never wear trousers.) Even areas in which to 'relax' sometimes saw a group of SAs huddled around one tiny electric heater and we couldn't always count on that.

I was very glad of my own thermals on one winter's day when, dressed as in-patients, several of us were obliged to cross a busy main road to reach the hospital set. Drivers must have thought that we'd escaped from somewhere and I was particularly sorry for one SA, whose operating gown left him in grave danger of indecent exposure. His mood was further soured later on by the fact that the runner who'd shepherded us across the road that morning was halfway through her own lunch before remembering that she should have collected us for ours. He demanded and was found a dressing gown for the return to the main studios.

I've often wondered what would have happened that day if I'd been knocked down and taken unconscious to a real hospital. Every detail of my role had been catered for, right down to a plastic wrist band with information that assigned me to the maternity department, which was a stretch of the imagination even then. As it was, I spent most of my time lying on a trolley, having been hoisted onto it by an SA who was a retired fireman, with occasional walks up and down the ward.

On the whole, the weather had to be really dire for a shoot to be called off. I remember fog so thick one day that we couldn't see across the set and driving rain on another that threatened to wash us all away. Thick snow descended on one occasion when we were preparing to shoot a fine spring morning. At least we were always still paid for turning up, although the drive home could be a nightmare. Here's another extract from my diary:

The journey to and from the unit base in the dark was gruelling, but I had a lot of fun in between. The shoot had been postponed from before Christmas, when snow stopped play, and at least one actor's holiday tan had to be subdued for continuity purposes.

Seated in the makeup van, I had my hair put up into 'victory rolls'. The village was supposed to be putting on some kind of wartime nostalgia celebration with a visit from Field Marshall Montgomery (Monty) himself. Dressed as veteran members of the Women's Land Army, another SA and I spent most of our time lining up in the street with members of the Home Guard, very youthful naval and army cadets (the genuine article in vintage uniforms) and most of the main cast.

There was a biting wind and it was so cold generally that we were issued with hand warmers to clutch. There was a lot of rain too, with the fringe benefit of sharing an umbrella with one of my favourite actors for some time. As daylight was short and the director didn't want to waste any of it taking everyone back to base for lunch, we were served in style in a nearby hotel. I had a very good baked Brie, fried potatoes and large salad, followed by a delectable sticky toffee pudding.

Last minute cancellations for reasons other than the weather were rare, although the offer of a day's work as a senior nurse was once withdrawn a few hours before I was due to arrive at the studio. I'd played the part of a hospital cleaner in a previous episode and it was thought that an eagle-eyed viewer might spot that and write in to complain about an unfeasibly rapid promotion. It was possible, I suppose, although I played many different parts in other shows and no one ever seemed to notice.

XVII
JOYFUL OR SAD OCCASIONS

Weddings, and more especially wedding receptions, were always fun to film. The atmosphere was generally buoyant and there were often perks in the way of fancy food that could actually be eaten. I once spent a wonderful afternoon seated at a long table and being entertained by an actor/director long considered to be a national treasure. It was a drama set in the early 1960s and, as well as occasionally slipping back into one of his best known comedic roles, he got us all to have a go at hand jiving. He was most anxious that everyone should be comfortable and enjoy their time on set, an attitude typical of a man I saw being equally considerate to everyone he worked with on other shows. A care worker told me once that he'd been just as kind to a learning disabled group that she'd taken on holiday. They'd come across him filming on an outdoor set and were thrilled when he called a halt just to chat to them and have photos taken.

Funerals were often shot out of sequence on a couple or more days. Clad in suitably sober attire, we might start off with the burial, sit through the service and then line up for the arrival of the hearse at the church. Orders of service booklets were meticulously prepared in case they appeared in close up and real undertakers were used for their professional demeanour and expertise in handling a coffin. Most of the time the actor who'd portrayed the character had simply moved on to other things, but sometimes an unexpected death had forced a change to the story line. There was great poignancy accompanied by genuine tears on those occasions, especially from people who'd been friends for years and already attended the real funeral. One morning while we were filming a wake, the actor delivering the eulogy broke down several times and kept apologising. It was very moving.

Over the years I saw a lot of evidence of bonding between the actors as well as those behind the camera and was present one day when a crew presented a huge chocolate cake to one of the veterans on his milestone birthday. We were out on location that day and I saw his surprise and delight, after which he insisted on sharing it round, even with a family of walkers who'd strayed onto the set. For the benefit of their young son, he went straight back into his role and chatted to him amiably through a mouthful of crumbs.

XVIII

WHEN THINGS WENT WRONG

All kinds of things happened to throw out carefully planned schedules, some of which could have been avoided but others not. A sudden death or illness, a major accident on the motorway or roadworks that had sprung up overnight causing long tailbacks forced directors to make last minute changes to the running order or employ stand ins where possible. Attitudes were less forgiving when someone had left it to the very last minute to travel to the location and then been thwarted by a sudden transport strike.

Such was the case one Monday morning when the lead actor in a busy scene crucial to the story line failed to appear. Not long after that, the character was written out. Coincidence? I couldn't say for sure, but I suspect not. When a show featured an ensemble cast rather than one main star, it was always a possibility and worth everyone minding their Ps and Qs. The same could be said of avoiding unsavoury incidents that might not go down well with those at the top of the food chain.

Fire alarms emptying a building on a few occasions or smoke coming out of a camera were minor inconveniences by comparison, as was the sudden realisation that an actor had gone through an entire scene with a script sticking out of his back pocket. A plan to feature a bus shelter was thwarted when it was discovered that birds were nesting in it.

Some incidents were amusing in retrospect, although not at the time. One that springs to mind is a sequence filmed in a real courthouse, to which we were driven in costume from the unit base. The poor chap playing the part of the judge was accosted by a member of the public when we emerged at the end of the day. It turned out that the man had a grudge against the judiciary and thought the actor the genuine article.

There was also the time that someone had forgotten to apply the fake blood to an 'injured' horse and it wasn't noticed until the scene was concluded and the tea break announced. It was back to square one then.

Occasionally one of the crew would have to stand in for someone who hadn't turned up and on one occasion things were so desperate that a crew member's boyfriend was roped in at very short notice to play the secret lover of one of the regular cast. The look of terror on the young man's face as he obeyed the instruction to sneak down the stairs and make a rapid exit from the hotel was quite genuine. Fortunately we were so far behind schedule that he only had to do it once.

Problems with lighting and camera angles often held things up. I once saw a hapless camera operator stuck up a tree after failing to capture a particularly elusive shot.

One of the funniest incidents I remember was when a small department store had been taken over for a period drama and had its windows decked out with vintage goods and prices to match. A scene was in full flow when a determined lady marched in looking for bargains. With so many people milling about, it took a while for the penny to drop that she wasn't meant to be there and even longer to persuade her to leave without the pedal bin she had her eye on.

XIX

PASSING THE TIME

Being an SA wasn't a good job for anyone who got bored easily. Once in a while I was either given the wrong call time or it was rearranged at the last minute, meaning that I arrived several hours before I was needed. Once in a while a whole day went by without my being called onto the set, which could be a little disappointing, although I was paid anyway. (I wasn't the one time that I was sent on the wrong day. Now that was annoying!)

As a writer, I often had a story to finish or edit and it was always interesting to meet new people, including a few who 'had been everywhere, knew everyone and had done everything'. Occasionally someone involved in amateur dramatics brought along a script and needed help to learn their lines. Most people came equipped with books or magazines and everyone had a wealth of anecdotes to relate, many to do with their experience of working on other shows. Others talked about their 'day jobs', which were many and various. Some SAs came from agencies specialising in police and security roles and even had their own uniforms. The memories of a veteran wrestler who is still heavily featured on YouTube were particularly enthralling. There were word games, quizzes and long discussions about current affairs. As long as we were kept warm and well fed, the time passed agreeably enough.

Sometimes we had to wait behind a set for a long time, with or without a monitor screen to keep us abreast with what was going on. I found a Kindle with its own built-in light very useful for those occasions. (It also allowed me to increase the size of the font on the many occasions that I'd forgotten my reading glasses.)

Only on one occasion did I find myself absolutely alone with nothing to read or do. A group of us booked just for the morning were already signing off when I was asked to stay behind. Something in one of the scenes we'd completed had caught the director's eye and he wanted to reshoot the segment in which I featured. Fortunately a kind member of the crew came to the rescue with an Agatha Christie novel and I'd read the whole thing by the time I was called.

The other time that I was the only SA booked, I'd been told in advance and was much better prepared. It was wonderful. I had a caravan all to myself at the unit base and even got to travel to the shooting location in style with the leading lady and the director.

XX

EXTRA MONEY

If scenes shot on one day involved changes of outfit and were scheduled for two or three episodes, we were generally paid more and there was also an overtime rate. (We got the basic rate for the whole day – nine hours – even if we were released much earlier.)

When I 'served' on juries, that was all eleven of us could expect. The 'foreman', on the other hand, who had a few words to say, was paid considerably more, elevated to the status of cast member, included in the credits and qualified for repeat fees. That had always been arranged in advance, though. Being given lines on the day was everyone's dream, but rarely happened.

However, doing considerably more than blending into the background did benefit me a few times. As a psychiatric nurse, for example, I had to join a team grappling with a highly disturbed patient. As an applicant for a housekeeping position, I demonstrated some domestic skills. At the vet's, my character actually had a name as well as a pet to look after.

Grey areas were sometimes left to the discretion of the AD responsible for signing everyone off and there were occasional disputes, but I didn't get involved in any of those.

It should be remembered that other production companies weren't bound by agreements between the BBC, ITV and Equity and could pay as much or as little as they chose. There were always people willing to work for next to nothing – or nothing at all – however much professional SAs might bemoan the fact.

XXI
HOW IT ALL ENDED FOR ME

In a word, Covid. Horror stories were abounding even before the first lockdown in 2020 and I decided not to accept any more bookings until the crisis was over. No one could have ever imagined how long it was going to continue. When the studios began to reopen, working conditions were far from the way that they had been before and I decided to call it a day.

Do I regret the decision? No. I miss the people, some of whom were part of my life for around twenty years, but not the long hours and all that driving in increasingly heavy traffic.

It was time to move on, but I still enjoy picking out familiar faces on screen and telling family and friends:

"I remember when…"

ABOUT THE AUTHOR

Born in Leeds, Maggie Cobbett ventured across the Pennines to study at the University of Manchester, and then taught French, German and EFL in the UK and abroad. Now settled with her family and cats on the edge of the Yorkshire Dales, Maggie takes inspiration from her writing from her surroundings, travels, family history – and of course, her work as a background artist.

Visit Maggie online at www.maggiecobbett.co.uk

OTHER BOOKS BY MAGGIE COBBETT

Treat yourself to a captivating read, or perhaps even a new career. All books available in print and Kindle editions.

Find out more at www.maggiecobbett.co.uk

NON-FICTION

EASY MONEY FOR WRITERS AND WANNABES

Your handy guide to writing 'fillers' for magazines and newspapers, and turning quick inspiration into profit.

NOVELS

SHADOWS OF THE PAST

Not far from Paris lies the village of Saint-André-la Forêt, where three English schoolgirls disappear without trace during the summer of 1965. Twenty years later, a stranded traveller stumbles across a skeleton in the nearby forest and ignores local people's warnings to leave well alone. The secrets she uncovers, some dating back to the darkest days of World War 2, are more than enough to put her own life in danger.

FORESHADOWING

A working holiday in France for so little? "It sounds too good to be true," says Daisy's mother, but her warning falls on deaf ears in this short prequel to 'Shadows of the Past'.

WHEELS ON FIRE

Wheelchair bound after a tragic incident, revenge is on Kaz's mind when she joins the school trip to Paris.

WORKHOUSE ORPHAN

Young orphan David is apprenticed to a Yorkshire coal miner, but what of the brothers and sister he has been forced to leave behind?

SHORT STORY COLLECTIONS

ANYONE FOR MURDER

A selection of murder mysteries to keep you guessing until the end.

HAD WE BUT WORLD ENOUGH

Life in a new country sounds exciting, but will these hopeful characters end up with more, or much less than they bargained for?

SWINGS AND ROUNDABOUTS

In fiction, as in life, things rarely work out as we expect – for characters, or readers...

Printed in Great Britain
by Amazon